A Better Day's Profits for the Retailer

A Better Day's Profits

E. W. Darrell, of Newton Centre, Mass., increased his business 400% within 14 months after he began to get a daily analysis of his efforts. He is now doing a business of over $4,000 a week, and gives most of the credit to accounts that account.

A Better Day's Profits

For The Retailer

Who Realizes that He Can Build
a Big Business Only by Getting
and Using all the
Small Facts

by

A. M. Burroughs

Burroughs Adding Machine Company

Detroit, Michigan, U. S. A.

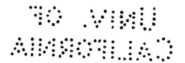

To the Reader:

THE object of this book is to illustrate the necessity of managing the retail store with open eyes. There are several *right* ways of doing most things, but the only *safe* way is to know, not merely *guess*, just what each day's work has produced in profit.

Before the book was sent to the printer, it was submitted to a recognized retail expert for his examination. We wanted outside criticism before we published the book. We wanted to know that it was right before we sent it out to retailers. Here is what he said:

"Referring to the manuscript sent to this office for criticism, I had several of our people go through it with an endeavor to find some place where we could find fault; but it seems as though we are unable to do so, as the several chapters, as you have them, certainly fit the purpose you have in mind in an elegant manner.

"In my opinion, you have touched upon many points that are overlooked in the conduct of the average retail store. Also that these points are forcibly analyzed and illustrated. I refer particularly to such chapters as "Weighing Employees," "What it Costs to Do Business," "Fixing Prices to Get a *Profit*," and "What a Sales Record Can Teach You."

"The points you have illustrated by sets of figures will not, in many instances, be *new* to retailers, but you have undoubtedly presented some of them in a *new light*. Retailers know a great many of the things you dwell upon; the fault is they don't *do* them."

You may know everything we have put in the following pages. We have reason to believe many retailers don't. Even, however, if you do know all we have told you, we have tried to put it in a new way and illustrated it with stories from actual retail life, that may be *interesting* as well as instructive.

If any part of the book is obscure—if you do not understand it—we may be able to lighten up the dark places. That is a part of our service—for which we make no charge.

Our main purpose is to help retailers find the most efficient way to run their business, conscious that when they have reached a greater efficiency, we as a Company will come into our share of the reward.

Burroughs Adding Machine Company
Detroit, Michigan

May 1, 1912

Contents

Richard F. Brune, now only 23 years old, came to this country eleven years ago with only $3 in his pocket. Three years ago he bought a store in Sawtelle, Cal., near Los Angeles. Scientific methods have enabled him to build up a business of $4,000 a week.

Cutting the Guess-Work out of Retailing

"Then and there I decided to govern my business from positive knowledge rather than from guess."

THE owner of a little drug store in San Francisco decided that there must be a reason for his store remaining small while other stores were getting big.

He set himself the task of finding the reason; of finding why it wasn't paying him; of finding what he needed to know to make it pay him the big profits he knew it ought to pay him.

"—Instead of one little Drug Store—"

He found the reason: Now instead of *one little* drug store he owns *seventeen big* drug stores.

Now he owns a fine automobile and a fine home. His check is good for anything he wants—he is making all kinds of money.

The United Cigar Stores Company, with its hundreds of stores and millions of capital, started from an "Analysis" of one little cigar store in Syracuse, New York.

"He now owns seventeen big Drug Stores."

If the owner of that little cigar store hadn't looked for and eliminated the weak places, he would never have built up the wonderful chain of stores which he now directs.

He asked himself what he needed to *know* about the business to eliminate the *blunders*; to make every move count for *bigger profits*.

By making his records show him what cigars *had sold*, he was soon able to buy cigars that sold *better*.

By making his records show him what cigars *had not sold*, he cut out the bad buying—the stocking up of cigars that he could not *sell*.

He found out how many smokers passed his store every day. Then he moved his store to a corner where *ten times* as many smokers passed it every day.

"—Studied the methods of his best clerks—"

He made his records show which of his clerks sold the *most* cigars at the *best profits*. Then he studied the *methods* of the *best* clerk and got more *like him* and less of the other kind.

He studied the attitude of his clerks towards the smokers who *came back*, and towards those who *didn't* come back. Then he changed the attitude of the clerks so that *nearly all* smokers came back.

He counted the seconds necessary to serve each smoker at the rush hour. Then he cut off half the seconds with little tricks of shortening steps. He arranged his display cases and his boxes so each clerk could reach every box from where he stood.

He counted the steps each smoker had to take inside the store. Then he arranged his display cases to cut out every unnecessary step.

He made it possible for each smoker to get a cigar while waiting for a car, hurrying to work, or to keep a business engagement.

The best cigars, the best clerks, the best store, all managed in the best way, laid the foundation for a chain of a thousand stores—for a corporation of many millions of dollars.

And the man who analyzed himself and his opportunities in that little Syracuse store, now directs that chain of a thousand stores.

A grocer in one of the suburbs of Boston was having a pretty hard fight with competition. The big Boston stores and two or three other live stores in his own town were getting the lion's share of the business.

"—he floated along—"

For eleven years he floated along, "wondering" how he could make more money.

At last things began to get so warm that he began to wake up and do more than just "wonder."

He decided he *had to find out why those big Boston stores were coming out into his territory and taking away his business,* while he was rapidly sliding down hill into the waiting arms of the sheriff.

These investigations were a revelation to him. He found that he was not the only Retailer in danger of bankruptcy.  He found *that 95% of all Retailers were just barely existing* and being gradually *forced out of business,*

"—reaching out into his territory—"

while a bare 5% were really *succeeding.*

Then he began to study the methods of the 5% who were succeeding. He found that those stores didn't use the hit and miss *guess-work* methods used by *unsuccessful* Retailers.

They were running their business from *positive knowledge.*

"Then and there," he says, "I decided that I would govern *my* business from *positive knowledge* rather than from accepted customs.

"I first asked myself what I wanted to know and decided as follows:

Which lines show a profit and how much?

What does it cost to obtain that profit?

Are my clerks earning more or less than I am paying them?

Are there any leaks and, if so, where?

"My bookkeeping system, which I thought was the *real thing*, didn't *answer* these questions, so I resolved to have one that would."

He got a system which gave him, is now giving him, the information he needed.

Then he found out how his business really stood. He learned what he needed to know to make himself a big manager.

He was able to bolster up the weak places, cut out the lines which were showing a loss, increase the lines which produced a profit, drop the clerks which were no good—*to do the things which paid.*

This was the business policy on which he made his appeal to the trade:

"1st. We know how to buy. The buying is divided among four from whom we expect, not theory but *actual* results. They must make good.

2nd. Our accounting system is simple but accurate and with *a positive mechanical* audit. It gives us the information which, combined with our skilled judgment, enables us to stop leaks and losses and handle a large volume of business at an exceptionally small expense. And we have no slow accounts or bad bills.

3d. We send no clerks out for orders. Do you realize what that saves? Telephone service is better and decidedly cheaper. We are glad to call you at your convenience.

4th. Our delivery system is so arranged as to eliminate idle or half filled teams. Deliveries made on regular schedule with *full* loads—not empty baskets but real sales.

All this means a saving of several thousands of dollars yearly. This saving we *deduct* from our selling price. We do not ask *you* to pay for bad bills, unnecessary and expensive methods or false motions. Why should you?"

Why, indeed?

Right business methods always appeal to Americans: this grocer has made his *method* of doing business pay for itself by advertising him.

P. A. Meyer & Sons of Erie, Pa., says the policy of "getting the facts" is "an eye-opener." "We know the exact condition of each department, and are able to act accordingly. There is no guess-work about it."

Managing With Your Eyes Open

Mere hard work will not bring success   There
must be behind the work a "know-how"
that will make it accomplish something.

A RETAIL hardware man kept himself so busy with
the little things of his business that he had no
time to make money.

But when he analyzed his methods, himself, his
business, to find the reason he wasn't making money,
he found he could unload half the petty work he was
doing onto a $3-a-week boy.

Then he began to understand that it was *his*
business, to *manage*, to *think*, to *plan* to find out *why*
things should be done, and *how* they *could* be done in
the best way.

He found that anybody could *do* the things that
had to be done if *he* told them *how*.

He quit using the brains, the enthusiasm, the
energy of his business for the office-boy duties.   He
devoted himself to the management of his business.

Now he is a merchant prince, the head of a great
hardware concern with an income several times bigger
than his *gross business* used to be.

A young German came to this country twelve
years ago at the age of 11, with but $3 in his pocket
and not a word of English in his vocabulary.

He obtained employment in a grocery store in
the German quarter of a New England city.   Here he
learned the grocery business.

Before he was 20 he was made manager of the store. When he was 21 he was appointed manager of a bigger Jersey City store. Now, at 23, he is manager of a $250,000 store in Illinois, with 75 employees.

If you would ask him how he succeeded, he would tell you that he always made it a point to *know the results of his efforts.*

. When he went into a new store, he wanted to know which lines of goods paid a profit and how much. And he wanted the information *all the time*, not merely for a few days.

He wanted to know whether one of the lines which wasn't moving, began to produce a profit when it was put "up front," and whether it continued to show a profit after it was put back to give some other slow line a chance.

He demanded records that showed him whether clerk No. 1 was producing a profit. When he found out which of the clerks produced the most profit, he used him as a standard for the other clerks—or their successors—to work up to.

A certain hardware dealer appealed to his jobber for a solution of a problem which he was wise enough to know was gradually pulling him down.

His business was increasing, much faster than his expenses, but at the end of the year he couldn't find the profit he thought he should have.

He had a good business. He was working hard, trying to plan and manage his business. He was a resourceful, industrious, clever merchant. Yet he wasn't making money.

When his jobber sent an accountant to go over his books, it

"—books didn't tell him—"

was found that his books didn't really tell him any-thing about his business. He kept accounts that didn't *account*.

He couldn't find out, for instance, whether it paid him to make a big window display of *pipe wrenches*, at a big discount off the marked price, to attract plumbers and gas fitters to his store.

He didn't know, for *sure*, whether his big assortment of *knives* was paying him.

In fact he didn't know *anything* for *certain*.

He was wasting his energies, his enthusiasm and his brains by planning and doing things that *never got him anywhere*.

With the aid of an accountant he put in a bookkeeping system which enabled him to get accurate reports on the *results* of each day's effort.

Then he was able to know, pretty quick, which line of effort produced the best results, the most *profits*.

Now the difference shows in his bank balance, and the fine home he owns—his business has more than quadrupled in two years.

Yet he is the same manager, in the same store, selling the same goods. He has just cut out the unprofitable methods.

He wasn't incompetent before. He is no better *manager* now. *He is just managing with his eyes open.*

"—with his eyes open—"

Wm. M. Brady, of Madison, Wis., conducts a store with his eyes
open. He provides himself with accounts that account. You can see
the difference in his bank balance.

Stretching the Capital

Study the methods of the banana man and the
peanut vender, who make a living on $10 capital.

A NORTHERN Indiana Furnishing Goods concern
went out of business a few months ago. When the
stock was inventoried
some caps were found
which were made es-
pecially for the Grant-
Colfax Presidential
Campaign in 1872.

Think of that!
Stock *forty years old.*

"—stock 40 years old—"

The caps cost about 25c each and there were three
dozen of them, costing $9 in all, wholesale.

Charge up a percentage equal to the cost of doing
business against that $9 worth of dead stock for forty
years and see what it *cost* the merchant to *keep it
on his shelves.*

Ask the banana man who stands at the corner of
Seventh Street and Franklin Avenue in St. Louis,
how much he could make on that $9 in forty years in
his business. Then you will know what it would
have profited this clothing concern had it *not* kept that
stock on the shelves—if it had used the capital right.

This banana man buys a cart load of bananas
every morning, costing him about $9, and sells them
before night for $20.

Since he works every day, holidays and Sundays,
he turns his capital every day, *30 times a month.*

On a capital of $9 he does a gross business of more
than $5000 in the nine months he is able to work.

In forty years he could do a gross business of $292,-000 on that little capital—without increasing his capital a single penny over that original $9.

What would he make if he had $9,000 capital and applied the same principles?

Any wonder the chain store fellows can keep buying more stores and undersell the "good-enough-for-me" one-man store?

The owner of a chain of six stores has never put a single dollar of his own money into the last four stores he opened.

When he opened his second store, he began buying in small quantities, stocking up every day and selling the goods before the bills came due.

In a short time he opened his third store, without putting any of his own money into it. Soon he increased his chain to six stores.

Now he is doing business almost entirely on the other man's capital. He buys in very small quantities and discounts his bills with the proceeds from the sales of the goods.

If the retailer provides himself with accurate and

complete detail information about his sales and his stock on hand, he can practically do business entirely on the capital of the houses from which he buys—and *make those houses glad to let him do it.*

Of course this is possible only by keeping such close tab on sales and purchases that the merchant can buy in very small quantities.

But isn't it better to stand the éxpense of adequate records and do a *big profitable* business on *little* capital, than to worry along without records and do a *small un*profitable business on the *most* capital you can rake and scrape?

"Small Capital rightly used may outweigh big Capital on the scale of profit"

George I. Kelly & Co., Clothiers, Hatters, and Furnishers, of Waltham, Mass., is a believer in modern accounting methods. They are making it pay.

Buying for Profit

**The goods it pays to handle
are the goods which go fast.**

A HABERDASHER in Chicago has built his business to the point where he averages a thousand sales a day in a little store 40 feet square—a gross business of more than $200,000 a year.

In this little store he keeps a wider variety of goods, and makes more real net profit, than most stores with five times his space and ten to fifteen times his capital and expense.

The secret of his success is in the small amount of stock which he carries and the frequency with which he turns his capital.

He plans to keep just one day's supply of stock on the shelves and in the

"—turning his Capital—"

show cases. Every night his stock is replenished just enough to replace the goods removed by the day's sales.

Accurate records for several years have enabled this merchant to know almost exactly how much he will sell of every line each day, and to make arrangements in advance for this sale.

He keeps a two weeks' supply of each line in his stock room on the fourth floor, where rents cost him very much less than he pays on the first floor.

Each night he sends down to the store just enough of each kind of stock for one day's business.

By knowing almost exactly how much goods he will be able to sell of each line, he is able to make quantity contracts with his jobbers on many lines, at quantity prices, with semi-monthly deliveries and monthly bills. He pays after he sells.

If his records show, for instance, that he will need 1,000 shirts of a certain size, his order to the jobber or manufacturer will be for 1,000 shirts, delivered in quantities of three dozen every other week.

Every month he gets a bill from the manufacturer or jobber for six dozen shirts. But, he has probably sold five dozen of them before the bill comes, so he can take the discount with money he has already received from the sale of the goods.

He invests $10 a week in salary for a young woman who gives her whole time to tabulating sales and expense figures.

The report this young woman gives him every day shows not only the number of sales for that day of every line of goods carried, but it shows also a comparison with the preceding day, the same day of the preceding week and the same day of the preceding year.

If you ask him, "How's business," he can tell you, for he *knows*. He doesn't *guess* at *his* figures.

It costs him $10 a week, a sum which would scare some retailers, but it enables him to do a gross business of *$4500 a week* on a capital that is less than some retailers use to do a business of *$100 a week*.

The Maypole Dairy Company, with 742 stores scattered all over England, handles its vast business in exactly the same way.

Every night each of the 742 stores telegraphs or telephones the exact amount of sales of each line to the home office in London.

The home office immediately ships to each store just enough goods to put the stock back where it was before the previous day's business.

When this Company opens a new store it puts $1,000 into carefully assorted stock, limited to the lines which experience has shown will sell readily. Then an amount is added each day to keep the total up to the original stock.

If, at the end of the day, the Manager wires that he has sold $500 worth of goods, his message giving the amount sold in each line, the home office will immediately ship him $500 worth of goods, bringing his total back to $1,000.

This wonderful chain of stores turns its capital more times in a week than the average retailer turns his capital in a year.

Starting with an original investment of $1,000, some of these stores do a business aggregating $200,000 a year—*one hundred and thirty or more complete turns of the original capital in a year.*

Every one of these stores is required to keep exact records of the sales of every kind of goods carried.

They are very simple records—just a number for each kind of goods and another number for the amount of each sale—but they are a wonder of completeness.

A certain cigar store in New York has one customer who likes a particular kind of cigar, the retail price of which is $4.75 a box.

This store keeps only two boxes of those cigars in stock. When this customer goes in and buys one of the boxes, which he does regularly every two weeks, another box is ordered. This keeps the stock always at two boxes.

On this one customer this one store does a gross business of $123.50, in one brand of cigars, with an investment of $6.50—supposing each box of cigars to cost $3.25 wholesale. This is about 13 complete turns of the capital invested.

If this store didn't keep records so that it could always know where it stood, it would likely buy a dozen boxes at a time—increasing the investment, reducing the number of times the capital could be turned, and letting the cigars get stale.

There is a chain of furnishing goods stores in St. Louis which, through careful buying, succeeded last year in turning its entire capital fifteen times.

This is an impossibility except under scientific management—which means simply the *keeping* and *using* of *facts* instead of theories.

"—where it can get quick delivery—"

This chain of stores buys all of its goods in St. Louis where it can get quick delivery and can buy in small quantities.

Some of the lines are turned every week; several more every month, and the entire capital at least fifteen times a year.

A big wholesale house in St. Louis estimates that fully 95% of all retailers overbuy. This wholesale house, unlike many others, urges its customers to buy in small quantities and buy often.

A bright salesman with his eye only on the *orders*, urges the retailer to stock up in anticipation of a raise in prices, or to get an extra 5% discount.

The overhead charge against the 11 dozen cans of tomatoes *on the shelves* which don't move, quickly eats up the 5% extra discount *on the 11 dozen,* and the 10% which the merchant makes on the *one* dozen he succeeds in *selling*.

If a merchant buys in very small quantities, he can't lose much if the goods *don't* move. If they *do* move, he has the money in hand with which to discount the bills when they come due.

The man who started in business with $5,000 and buried half of it in the ground, was better off than the man who buries half his capital in dead stock which don't move.

The man who buried his money in the ground didn't pay the profits he made on the other half to keep it in the ground; the man with half his capital in dead stock has to pay rent and all of his cost of doing business to keep this dead stock on the shelves.

Louis Meyer, meat and provisions, in Brooklyn, N. Y. Meyer now employs several butchers and operates a wholesale department. Every day he gets a statement of the business done and keeps in remarkably close touch with his extensive business.

Stopping Store Leaks

"If you had a barrel of molasses out in the warehouse which was leaking, when would you want to know about it, the first day, or at the end of the year?"

Over-weight and Over-measure

FOOD Inspector Ottesen of Iowa, while checking weights and measures at Waterloo, Iowa, found five grocers whose scales gave over-weight.

These five pairs of scales, Ottesen said, "long weighted" each of these grocers out of hundreds of dollars every year.

One grocer was selling about 50 lbs. of lard a day, at ¼ ounce over-weight. This one leak, on one kind of goods, aggregated about $40 a year.

Bad Buying

The average retailer is a poor buyer. Ninety percent of all retail stores over-buy. The biggest store leak is in the failure of the retailer to turn his capital often.

He should keep accurate records, through the use of duplicate sales slips, or other means, of all sales. Then he will not be likely to duplicate the mistake, even if he doesn't prevent it the first time.

A jobber's discount of *50%* from list price is a loss if the goods will not sell. The retailer must not buy for the *extra discount*, but for the *profit*.

Incompetent Help

Every employee in the retail store should be put on a merit basis. The clerk who isn't able to sell goods at a profit is incompetent and unprofitable to the store. Keeping him is like letting the faucet remain open in the *vinegar* barrel—only it is *profits* and not *vinegar* which are leaking.

Loss of Goods from Stock

A big New York store, doing a business of $10,000,-000 a year, estimates that 2% of its sales, or $200,000, is stolen from the store every year. If this same proportion of goods is stolen from the average retail store, then the store doing a business of $50,000 a year would lose $1,000 through theft of goods from stock.

A Shop Lifter

Failure to Charge Goods Sold on Credit

When a sale is made on credit and no record is made of it, the retailer stands to lose the profit he should make on the sale; the time which has been invested in the buying; the time invested in the selling of the goods; the cost of the labor of handling the goods; the cost of keeping them on the shelves, and several other losses, including the big loss which the carelessness will cause in other work.

Wasteful Bookkeeping

It costs more money sometimes to keep incomplete records in an unsystematic way, than it would cost to keep complete records in the right way.

The bookkeeping system should be up-to-date. It should be carefully worked out by experts. It should be especially designed for the store. It should give the exact information needed, as economically as possible.

Errors in Adding Figures

The amount of money lost in the average store every year through mistakes in figures is enormous.

A Customer gets his bill. It is a little *less* than he expected, but he thinks possibly he made a mistake. He pays on your figures.

If it happens to be a little *more* than he expected he asks you about it, and *you* spend some *valuable time* finding the error and correcting it.

If you make a mistake in your figures you are sure to lose, whether it is against you or against the other fellow.

Figuring Profits Wrong

A recent investigation conducted by the Burroughs Adding Machine Company, showed that fully 75% of all retailers figure profits on a basis which gives them 3% to 8% less than they think they are getting, often figuring themselves out of any profit.

This is the vital end of a business. What is the use to sell goods, if profit, the whole purpose of selling, is lost in bad methods of figuring prices.

Failure to Charge All Expenses

All expenses are going to come out of the gross profits whether they are put down as a part of the cost of doing business or not.

If a man pays out $20 a month for rent, he will not find it to his credit in the bank at the end of the year, even if he doesn't charge it into the expense of doing business.

The same applies to every kind of expense in the business. Every one of the leaks mentioned in this chapter is an expense, whether you charge it as such or not.

It is better to err on the side of too liberal charging of expenses and find an unaccounted for balance in the bank, than to find a puzzling deficit caused by not charging all your expenses. The deficit may disable you just when failure to pay a big bill means bankruptcy.

Failure to Discount Bills

If a retailer turns his capital every week and discounts all his bills at 2%, the clean profit from this source alone amounts in a year to a sum greater than his capital—52 times 2% is 104%. If he doesn't take the discount, he loses it, of course.

Unsystematic Delivery

A grocer in a New England town was maintaining nine delivery wagons at a cost of about $200 a week.

By applying better methods to his delivery, he was able to cut the number of wagons from nine to three, stopping a leak of $125 a week—$6500 a year.

Wrong Deliveries

It costs from five to ten cents to deliver every order sold. If from ten to fifty mistakes are made every day in deliveries, a leak of from $200 to $1,000 a year will result. The loss in customers may increase this sum enormously.

Presents, Donations, Etc.

Possibly some of this is necessary. Some retailers make it a matter of considerable expense. It is a leak which should be carefully watched.

If a retailer gives away an amount equal to only 1% of his gross sales in that way, he stands to lose $500 a year on every $50,000 a year of gross business.

Wasted Time

 A grocer hired a man capable of selling $200 worth of goods a week. Bad management wasted half his time and he only sold $100 worth a week. The grocer lost the profits on a gross annual business of $5,200 —$100 a week.

When you hire a clerk, you simply buy a certain amount of his time, to be used as you direct. If you direct wrong, or he wastes part of his time, you lose.

Time can be wasted in a thousand ways. Most of these are under the control of the employer.

Most of the waste of time is caused by bad methods controlled by the owner of the store.

The Reduced-Price Leak

When goods are marked to sell at $1.00 and it is necessary for any reason to cut off 10%, the reduction from the marked price represents a loss.

If the cut is necessary to make the goods sell, it is a loss due to bad buying. It also produces another loss by giving customers the impression that the original price allowed an enormous profit.

Wasteful Advertising

One retailer used space two columns, ten inches deep, in his weekly paper to run a poorly worded and poorly arranged announcement. It cost him $200 a year and produced almost nothing.

A competitor used half as much space and changed his advertisement every week, using strong selling arguments. He doubled his business in two years.

Advertising, properly directed, is one of the most productive expenditures of the modern retail store, but misdirected advertising can be very wasteful, or even harmful.

Extravagance in Lighting

One retailer cut the cost of his lighting in half and at least doubled the efficiency of his lighting system by studying the arrangement of his lights. The proper lighting system puts just the right amount of light where it is needed.

Arrangement of Store

In a certain store each clerk had to walk all over the store to wait on customers. A re-arrangement of the store stopped this and cut out about two hours wasted efforts for each clerk each day—about $600 worth of time in a year, considering the several clerks. This time, which cost money, was profitably used.

Arrangement of Goods

A stationer was making a big display of scratch pads for school children the day before school opened. When he came in from lunch he stopped to look into the window, and noticed the absence of pencils. Immediately he went in and caused a pencil to be placed alongside each pad.

This suggested the connection between other goods. On investigation he found that scores of items were not in their proper place in the store. He had them placed where the customer who bought one item would see many others that he might need in the same line. This saved much walking for the clerks and helped each kind of goods to sell others.

Store Alterations

Special sales, special displays of goods, the rearrangement of departments and offices, repairs, etc., cause numerous little carpenter jobs in the store.

These little jobs are the source of a considerable leak.

Some carpenters can put a lot of time on a little job, and, if the changes are not properly timed, employees of the store are often compelled to waste much of their time, paid for by the store.

Extravagant Use of Supplies

Sales books, report blanks, office stationery, statement forms, blank books and pens, ink, pencils, etc., cost a neat little sum in a year. A big saving can be effected by proper care and a leak is pretty apt to follow lax methods.

Careless Packing of Goods

Goods which have to be delivered to customers require care in packing. Much merchandise is damaged or entirely spoiled

Wasteful Packing

by poor packing. Some money is wasted in the course of a year through the use of bigger boxes than is necessary and through the waste of time in packing—time which is paid for with good money and which, if saved, could be used for other work.

Lost Containers

Baskets, boxes, egg crates, etc., used in delivering goods, cost money. The number lost during the year usually amount to a serious leak.

Wasted Twine, Paper Bags, Etc.

Even in little stores the cost of wrapping paper, twine, paper bags, boxes, etc., amounts in a year to a neat sum. A careless employee can easily cut a big slice off the profits by a wasteful use of these supplies.

Clerk's Mistakes

Clerks, working at small salaries, are usually careless, inefficient and thoughtless. They make enough mistakes any time, but when tired they make more.

Unless they work under the direction of a system which makes their work pretty near mechanical, and a close check is kept on their mistakes, they will likely do as much harm as good.

Dissatisfied Customers

A regular customer is worth from $10 to $50 a year to the average retail store. Some customers are worth a great deal more, some a great deal less.

It is very easy to drive customers away. Sometimes it is hard to get them. It is easy to lose a big amount of money through the careless handling of customers.

Breakage and Spoilage of Merchandise

A careless employee will spoil a very large amount of merchandise in a year, cutting deep into the profits. Even a careful employee is pretty sure to spoil some.

Depreciation of Merchandise

Certain goods shrink in weight; others in size. These facts must be taken into consideration both in buying and in selling. Don't buy too much. Be sure the selling price covers the loss of shrinkage.

Bad Accounts

To be sure of collections, the merchant must have accurate and complete records. The slow-pay customer may not remind you if you forget his bill.

If he asks you for a statement some day, when he has the money, and you can't give him the exact figures at once, then its your loss if he spends the money for a vacation trip.

Leaks in Your Business

The leaks suggested here, apply to your business. Some of them may cause you only a little loss. Some may be swallowing about all your profits.

A retailer, who is not now in business (we'll call him Smith) fooled himself, for a time, into thinking that he wasn't losing anything through leaks in his store. He refused to see the leaks.

"I watch things pretty close," he said, "and I know just what it costs *me* to run *my* business. Jones, down the street, is a crank on digging out expenses to charge up against his business. Not for me!"

Jones has the exclusive business for his section now, and is a very prosperous retailer. The sheriff closed out Smith's business over a year ago.

Remember this: All leaks and other expenses in your business have to be paid at their full face value, whether you see them or not.

If the sheriff gets your business, don't let it be said that he got you because you *guessed* at your expenses.

What it Costs to Do Business

A retailer may fool himself by failing to charge all of his expenses into his cost of doing business, but his expenses will come out of his gross profits just the same.

UNTIL recently retail grocers in a certain Western city were paying $1.40 for a 50-pound sack of flour, which they were selling for $1.55. This allowed them a gross profit of only fifteen cents per sack.

The Retailer Grocers' Association in this Western city took up this problem in a special convention. Most of the grocers agreed that this fifteen cents did not allow a profit, though a few were of the opinion that they were making a little on it.

The result of the discussion was an investigation into the cost of doing business in that city. When the different grocers began producing their books to show their expenses, a very wide range of costs were shown.

"--average cost 15 per cent!--"

Some of them had cost systems and declared it cost them 22% to 25% to do business. A few, while admitting that their systems were not very complete, estimated their costs at 10% to 12%.

The final result of the investigation was an agreement (Those who *knew* didn't "agree.") upon the average of 15% as the proper and correct cost of doing business.

But this average was plainly incorrect because the low figures ranging around eleven and twelve and thirteen percent were from the stores of grocers who did not figure to make anything over a reasonable salary for themselves; who did not figure to make anything on the investment in the store buildings they happened to own; who did not figure for interest on their investments, and who overlooked a score or more important items that should be included in the expenses.

The high percentages, ranging around twenty to twenty-five percent, were from the stores of retailers who had applied a searching cost system to their business. These merchants were charging up to their business every item that could be considered as expense and it made their expenses seem high.

The investigators took these high percentages, which were about correct, and the low percentages, which were eight or ten to fifteen percent too low, and combined the whole list to arrive at the *average* of *fifteen* percent. Now a good many retailers who think they are fixing prices right, are puzzling over their failure to find the profit they expected last year.

The cost of doing business is, of course, just the same whether a merchant includes all of the items or only a few of them in his expense account.

The only difference is that he deludes himself into thinking that the cost of doing business is only 15% when in reality it probably is 20% to 25%.

If he fools himself in this way, and figures for a 10% profit, the chances are that the expenses and the extra cost of doing business, *which he hasn't*

"—holding the sack—"

figured into his percentages, will eat up that profit, and leave him holding the sack at the end of the year.

A Cleveland grocer thought he was clearing $100 a month, $1200 a year, over and above his expenses.

But the $100 a month included his own salary, the interest on his investment, the salary of his wife who spent most of her time in the store, and a number of other items.

If the grocer had allowed himself interest on his investment, that alone would have produced $50 a month without risk or worry.

Another $25 a month of his "profits" rightly came out as expenses incurred in running the store. He had charged several expense items as "investment."

Instead of making $100 a month clear, he was not only failing to make anything, but he and his wife were both working for almost nothing.

If they had both worked in some other store they might have earned $100; so instead of making $100 they were losing $100 a month.

A grocer in Pittsburg was interested in politics. Last year he succeeded in landing a city job, paying him $2,500 a year.

When he got this job he decided to sell his store. He placed the store in the hands of a broker, and had an accountant go over the books to place a value on the stock and to see what the business was worth.

The Accountant's report showed that no charge had been made for salaries.

" —The family helps—"

41

The grocer, his wife and four children run the store. When proper allowance was made for salaries, the store was found to be paying a fraction over one-half of one percent a year on the investment.

Instead of a fairly profitable business, one salable at a premium for good will, it was found to be a business so nearly *un*profitable as to be unsalable.

Fixtures and stock were finally sold at a loss. Nothing was received for good will, because there was no good will—only a chance to work for nothing and take the ordinary business risks besides.

In scientifically managed stores it has been found that the salaries of the clerks average around nine percent of the gross sales by those clerks.

The salaries of managers, bookkeepers and other employees, who do not sell, run the average cost for salaries up to about thirteen to thirteen and a half percent of the gross sales.

Rent is likely to average around four percent, delivery around one and a half to two percent, light and heat from one to two percent, and so on down the list of expenses.

No merchant, as he so frequently does, should *assume* these percentages to be his costs. He should get his own costs from his business, considering these percentages only as standards by which to judge whether he is higher or lower than the average.

The merchant who would know his cost of doing business should classify his expenses into such accounts as will give him the information he needs.

"—searching out expenses—"

He should install a cost system that will search out all of the expenses and enable him to know, not merely a *few* of the things which he pays for, but *all* of the things which enter into his cost of doing business.

Here is a list of the expenses used by one wide-awake Merchant:

Rent—If the building is leased; depreciation or upkeep if it is owned.

Salary—of all employees, and the manager.

Delivery Expense—including repairs to wagons, harness, shoeing of horses, grease, feed, barn, rent, etc.

Light—including light in barns, etc.

Heat—including coal, fireman, etc.

Ice—for drinking fountains, refrigerators, soda fountains, etc.

Advertising—in newspapers, circulars, etc.

Printing—stationery, blank books, bill heads, etc.

Gifts—presents, donations, etc.

Telephone and telegraph tolls.

Insurance—stock, fixture, burglar, etc.

Taxes—on fixtures, stock, etc.

Interest—Paid out.

Paper Bags—wrapping paper, twine, etc.

Breakage and spoilage of goods.

Repairs—on fixtures, etc.

Depreciation on merchandise.

Shrinkage of merchandise.

Depreciation on fixtures, furniture, etc.

Bad Accounts.

Goods stolen from stock.

Depreciation from cost price by change of style and by the purchase of unsalable stock which makes it necessary to reduce prices.

Some merchants add freight and cartage to this list but it should not be charged as an expense. It is a part of the original cost of the goods and should be charged to goods and not to expense.

The National Association of Credit Men recommended the following rules for figuring costs and profits.

1. Charge interest on the net amount of your total investment at the beginning of your business year, exclusive of real estate.

2. Charge rental on all real estate or buildings owned by you and used in your business at a rate equal to that which you would receive if renting or leasing it to others.

3. Charge in addition to what you pay for hired help an amount equal to what your services would be worth to others; also treat in like manner the services of any member of your family employed in the business not on the regular pay roll.

4. Charge depreciation on all goods carried over on which you may have to make a less price because of change in style, damage, or any other cause.

5. Charge depreciation on buildings, tools, fixtures, or anything else suffering from age or wear and tear.

6. Charge amounts donated or subscriptions paid.

7. Charge all fixed expenses, such as taxes, insurance, water, lights, fuel, etc.

8. Charge all incidental expenses, such as drayage, postage, office supplies, livery or expenses of horses and wagons, telegrams and telephones, advertising, canvassing, etc.

9. Charge losses of every character, including goods stolen or sent out and not charged, allowance made customers, bad debts, etc.

10. Charge collection expense.

11. Charge any other expense not enumerated above.

12. When you have ascertained what the sum of all the foregoing items amounts to, prove it by your books, and you will have your total expense for the year; then divide this figure by the total of your sales, and it will show you the per cent which it has cost you to do business.

13. Take this percent and deduct it from the price of any article you have sold, then subtract from the remainder what it cost you (invoice price and freight), and the result will show your net profit or loss on the article.

14. Go over the selling prices of the various articles you handle and see where you stand as to profits, then get busy in putting your selling figures on a profitable basis and talk it over with your competitor as well.

Fixing Prices to Get a *Profit*

"Nine-tenths of all retailers are making
less than they think they are. They are
always surprised when they find it out."

A RETAIL hardware store in a small Wisconsin
town, had been dragging along for several years,
supposedly making a profit.

Three differ-
ent men had
gone into part-
nership with the
original owner
and after a year
or so had with-
drawn, leaving
a part of their
capital behind them as "pay" for the "experience."

CAPITAL
SUNK

The fourth partner was a young accountant who had
spent a year in the accounting department, and another
year in the selling department, of a city store.

When he formed the partnership in the Country
store, he determined to find out just how things stood—
though he didn't know the store had already frozen out
three partners.

He soon learned that most of the hardware man's
profits were imaginary. While the sales ran to a nice
figure, the profits were mostly on paper.

His trouble was that while estimating his cost of
doing business as a certain percentage of the gross
business, which is the *selling* price, he added this same
percentage to the *cost* price when figuring the selling
prices of individual items.

He knew that the percentage of his expenses was figured on the gross business, but he didn't realize that a percentage of the gross business is *more* than the same percentage of the invoice cost.

If you figure your cost of doing business as a percentage of your gross business, you must, of course, allow that much of your selling price for cost of doing business.

When you sell $1 worth of goods, you say that a certain percent of that is profit, a certain percent goes for cost of doing business and the balance is for the cost of the goods.

Take some item in your stock and deduct the two percentages from the selling price you have established and see if you still have the cost price left.

"—taking part of each dollar—"

Your profits and cost of doing business come out of the dollar you take in—not out of the 60 or 70 or 80 cents you pay out for the article.

If you buy a pair of shoes for $2 and sell them for $3, your profit comes out of the $3—not the $2. The profit can only come out of the *selling* price.

Get that straight—when the $2 is invested in the pair of shoes, *it is gone*. There is no $2 anymore. There is no money at all—nothing but a pair of shoes.

If you don't *sell* the shoes, there will never be any profit. But if you *do* sell the shoes, you have $3 or whatever you sell them for—you never see the $2.

Since you have nothing left but the $3, your profit can *only* come out of that. Everything comes out of the $3. Nothing can come out of the $2. That

46

goes to pay for the goods. The $1 left after the goods are paid for is a part of the $3.

In the hardware store referred to goods were marked by adding what was really a percentage of the *selling* price to the *cost* price.

This mixing of methods resulted in a loss, except on a few articles which permitted a very high percentage of profit.

Where there was competition on an article, 18% *of the cost price* was added for cost of doing business, and 10% of the cost price, was added for profit.

This net profit of 10%, looked good "on paper," but that was the only place it could be found. It wasn't in the cash drawer. It never got into the bank. The manager never saw it *in money*.

The real cost of doing business was 22% instead of 18%. Part of the expenses had been figured as investment. Other items had not been included at all.

If you think he *could* make a profit on that basis, try to figure it out. Add 28% to $1; then subtract 22% from the selling price it gives you.

Adding 28% to $1 gives you  $1.28. 22% of $1.28 is 28.2 cents. His real cost of doing business, 22%, taken from the *selling* price, amounted to *more* than his 28% added to the *cost* price.

A Michigan grocer did a gross business of $20,000 last year. His cost of doing business, includ-

"—take out all costs—"

ing spoilage of goods, etc., was $4,600, or 23%, and he figured for 10% net profit.

His purchases during the year aggregated $15,000. To this he added, in the process of marking each item during the year, the gross profit he wanted to make, 33%, making the goods sell at $20,000.

His banker asked him recently how much profit he made last year. He said $2,000—10% on his $20,000 gross business.

He made the mistake of assuming that 33% added to his *cost* was the same as 33% of his *selling* price.

Let's see how far he was wrong; 33% added to $15,000 makes $19,950. (He evidently added a little more than 33% to some items.) 33% taken from $20,000 leaves $13,400.

If he paid $15,000 for the goods he sold for $20,000, and his cost of doing business was $4,600, his net profit was only $400. $400 is only 2% on $20,000.

If your profit is to *come out* of the *selling* price, and *not* out of the *cost* price, it is plain that the *percentages* should be *figured* on the *selling* price.

In the hardware store referred to they handled a certain kind of stove which was also handled by a competitor. The wholesale price was $9.25, and the freight and cartage were 75 cents, making the stove cost $10, set down in the store.

Competition was very keen on this stove and it was decided to cut the profit to 10% net. So 18% of the cost was added for cost of doing business and 10% for profit, making the stove sell at $12.80.

The hardware man thought he was making a profit of $1. Let us see what the new partner, an accountant, showed him:

The real cost of doing business, as already explained,

was 22% instead of 18%, but the accountant figured it first on the 18% to illustrate the principle.

If the article cost $10 and it was desired to make 28% gross profit, we must consider the selling price as 100%, and the cost price as 72%, or all of that 100% except the gross profit of 28%.

Now if $10 is 72% of the selling price, the selling price must be $13.89.

Here is the way to work it out:

Selling price........................100%
Cost to do business...........18%
Profit desired................10%   28%
Wholesale cost...................... 72%

$13.888 *Answer*

Cost price, in percentage, .72)$10.0000 Cost in money.

astonished

```
                          7 2
                          ‾‾‾
                          2 80
                          2 16
                           640
                           576
                           ‾‾‾
                           640
                           576
                           ‾‾‾
                            64
```

Selling price, $13.89.

Reducing the problem back, to prove it, we have:

$13.89 Selling price.
   .28 Percentage.
‾‾‾‾‾‾
 111.12
 277 8
‾‾‾‾‾‾‾
$3.88 92 Gross profit in dollars.

$13.89 Selling price.
  3.89 Gross profit.
‾‾‾‾‾
$10.00 Cost price.

From this it seems clear that the selling price should have been $1.09 higher than it was, to allow 10% net profit, after allowing 18% for cost of doing business.

In reality it took $2.30 of the $2.80 gross profits to cover the 18% cost of doing business.

But his *real* cost of doing business was 22%, instead of 18%. So the cost price should have been but 68% of the correct selling price. (22% and 10% subtracted from 100% leaves 68%.)

Figuring the same as before, $10 is 68% of *$14.70*, which is *$1.90* above the price at which the stoves were actually sold.

Taking 22% out of $14.70 for cost of doing business and 10% for profit leaves almost exactly $10.

Practically all merchants figure their cost of doing business as a percentage of the gross sales, the *selling* price. Yet a large percentage of them figure as if this were a percentage of the *cost* price.

Changing the base of figuring is dangerous. It fools Retailers into thinking they are getting more profit than they really are. Here is a case which illustrates that point.

A certain clothier, who was figuring for 30% net profit, planned a special "25% off" sale. He thought he would still make 5% net, and could afford to sacrifice part of his profit for advertising purposes.

Suits marked to sell at $20 were reduced 25%, or chopped down to $15.

These suits cost $13.50. Twenty percent was added for cost of doing business and 30% for profit, making the selling price a fraction over the $20.

Twenty percent cost of doing business on the original marked price ($20) is $4. Adding $4 to $13.50 (cost price) gives us $17.50. So when he sold that suit at $15 he actually *lost* $2.50.

During the sale he disposed of $3,000 worth of

clothing—*at a loss of* $500 *in cash.* Yet he *thought* he was making 5%, or $1.50.

He was all right as long as he added 50% to his cost price, though it allowed him less profit above his cost of doing business than he thought, but when he began cutting prices, he ran into unseen danger.

Add 50% to $13.50. Then deduct 50% from the new price. You lose $3.38 in the operation.

Apply this to some of *your* prices.

This method of arriving at selling prices differs slightly from the regular methods of figuring percentages. We have found that while the regular percentage method is correct, many people fail to remember that a percentage added to the cost of goods is less than the same percentage of the price thus marked.

Adding 10% to the invoice cost of an article, allows 10% profit on the 70 or 80 cents you *pay* for the goods and not 10% of the dollar in the cash drawer.

If it were convenient to arrive at percentages on a basis of the cost price, and to always remember that the percent of profit *added to the cost* price is always a profit *on* the *cost* price and *not* a percentage of the money *taken in* then the old percentage method would be fine.

Here are two views of H. A. Ballou's up-to-the-minute paint store in Worcester, Mass. A girl keeps the records which show Mr. Ballou just what he accomplished yesterday as compared with the same day last week, last month and a year ago.

What a Sales Record Can Teach You

"It is by knowing what *has* sold, that the chain store fellows are able to make such enormous sales on such a small stock."

THE banana man who sells his entire stock of bananas every night can tell you the exact number of bananas purchased and the exact number sold during any business day.

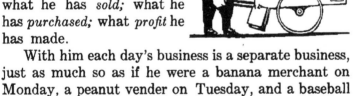

He knows all there is to know about the "sales end" of his business. It isn't *guess work* with *him*. He knows absolutely what he has done; what he has *sold;* what he has *purchased;* what *profit* he has made.

With him each day's business is a separate business, just as much so as if he were a banana merchant on Monday, a peanut vender on Tuesday, and a baseball player on Wednesday.

If he overbuys, he just cuts the price to make his stock move. He doesn't carry any dead stock. It isn't necessary to take an inventory at the end of the day to find out how much stock he has. He has *none*.

What he doesn't know about his *sales* and *purchases* isn't worth bothering about.

He has a "statement of his business" that makes him look like a wizard compared to most retailers.

He has *sales analysis* down to a fine point.

Yet the banana man doesn't need to keep books.

53

He has only one line of goods; he is his own and only clerk; he closes out his business every day—it is comparatively simple to arrive at all the sales facts.

But even the smallest retailer has a much more complicated business.

The average retailer has many lines of goods. He has several clerks. He doesn't close out his business every day. It continues from day to day, week to week and month to month. He doesn't even close it out at the end of the year.

On account of its being *bigger*, he can't know as much about his business unless he uses *bigger methods* for getting the information.

If a man has a mind *big* enough and *magic* enough and *superhuman* enough to grasp all the details of a big retail business and to store them up in his memory for weeks and months—

Well, then, he would be *wise enough* to use records instead of brain cells for a bookkeeping system

He would do just what all the successful retailers, the chain store fellows, and the really successful one-man businesses are doing.

There is a chain of big clothing stores, doing business in a number of cities, employing from twenty-five to a hundred clerks in each store, which can give you just as complete information about its sales as can the banana merchant who sells but one line of goods, has but one clerk, and who closes out his business every day.

This chain store company is not unusual; its methods are unusual only in that they are typical of the methods of other *successful* merchants in every line of business.

For every sale that is made in each of the stores in this chain, the clerk makes out a sales slip giving the name and amount of the goods sold and the price.

The bookkeeper tabulates this information and is able to tell at the end of the day how much goods of each line has been sold, the number and the amount of the sales by each clerk, the number and the volume of sales in each department, and number and the volume of sales in the entire store.

In the home office, the bookkeeper tabulates this information so that the managers of the great corporation which conducts the stores can tell at a glance exactly what profit has been produced by each line of goods, and by each clerk in each store.

If the expenses in each store, for instance, exceed by one-fourth of one percent the established average on the total sales, that store is going to hear from the Home Office before long.

Each store is allowed about 10 to $10\frac{1}{2}\%$ of its total sales as salaries. After the Managers' salary in each store is taken out and allowance made for bookkeepers, stenographers, janitors, watchmen, etc., about $8\frac{1}{2}\%$ to 9% is left to pay the clerks.

Home Office tabulates sales from branch office records

If a single clerk shows sales in such small amount as to raise the percentage represented by his salary to above 9%, he will very quickly hear from the Manager.

If the condition continues for any considerable length of time, the clerk is certain to be dropped and some one else put in his place who can reduce the cost of sales behind his counter to 9% or less.

If a clerk sells enough goods to bring the

percentage represented by his salary down to less than 8% of his sales, the management watches him and soon raises his salary or promotes him.

And then if a certain line of collars, for instance, doesn't sell as readily as some other line, the line which sells best, (the store is in position to *know* what lines sell best) will soon be the only line of collars carried— the line which will be pushed.

With complete sales information these stores are able to quickly eliminate the goods which *won't* sell and to replace them with goods which *will* sell.

And no store which doesn't keep a complete record, and which doesn't *push* lines which show a fair profit and *drop* lines which don't, can long hope to compete with stores like those in this chain.

Apply these methods to your business for a while and see if you don't increase your sales and decrease your ratio of expenses.

Figuring Stock Turnovers

"Business is a tank of profits. Capital is a myriad of sponges. The sponges should be constantly put into the tank one at a time, then taken and squeezed dry."

A SHOE dealer bought ten pairs of shoes at $2 a pair and sold them at $3 a pair, costing him $20 and selling for $30. He turned his capital *once*, at 33 1-3% gross profit on the selling price.

An implement dealer bought a wheelbarrow at $2 and sold it for $3. Then he bought and sold another and another and another until he had sold ten, costing him $20 and selling for $30.

"—turning capital often—"

He turned his capital *ten times*, at 33 1-3% on the selling price at each turn.

One merchant makes 33 1-3% on his investment. The other makes 333 1-3%, gross.

The difference is that one man invests $20 *once*. The other man invests $2 *ten times*. Both do a gross business of $30.

If both had $20 at the start, the Implement Dealer could have invested his other $18 in a dozen other items. By the time the Shoe Dealer had sold his whole ten pairs of shoes the Implement Dealer would have sold *ten each* of the other twelve items.

Capital is turned *once* when it is invested in stock and all the stock is sold.

In practice this becomes very complicated, because a part of the capital invested is released almost immediately and put back into additional stock.

"—turned capital once—"

This has the apparent effect, on the books, of increasing the investment. The purchase records show stock purchases very much in excess of the capital invested. Sales records show, however, that this stock has been sold.

A Dry Goods man doing $100,000 business per year on a $10,000 investment, for instance, probably puts $60,000 to $70,000 into stock—that is, re-invests his $10,000 capital from six to seven times.

Knowing the amount of money originally invested, the average amount of stock on hand and the total amount of the purchase, the Retailer can arrive at the number of times he has turned his capital without reference to the amount of the gross business. Whether he has turned it at a profit each time is another matter.

We have purchased $30,000 worth of goods. Our stock averaged $5,000. Our original investment was $5,000.

We have re-invested our money six times. We still have the same amount of stock we had in the beginning. So we have invested our capital six times.

The hardware man who has $10,000 worth of stock when he takes his inventory needs to know the *amount of the purchases* and the average stock on hand to arrive at the number of his turnovers.

When he tries to figure the number of turnovers on the gross business, he must allow for the profit on each turn of his capital *before he can know the number of turnovers.* He is working without a starting point.

If he knew the amount of the purchases and the average amount of stock on hand, it would be an easy matter to see that he has re-invested the amount represented by his stock a certain number of times.

Suppose you had a gross business of $10, had stock on hand worth $1, and knew that you averaged $1 worth of stock during any given period, how many times would you have turned the stock investment of $1?

Most retailers would jump to the conclusion that you had turned it ten times.

Now, let's see. Suppose you made 50% gross profit (based on selling price) at each turnover. Fifty percent of $10 is $5, so your total stock investment represented in the $10 gross business was only $5.

You turn your capital *once* when *you sell all the goods you have bought,* regardless of the price at which the goods are sold.

The Robinson & Jones Co., of Natick, Mass., are dealers in coal, wood, brick, lime, grain, etc., and operate a grain elevator in connection. A daily report of business done, keeps the manager of this company in perfect touch with the varied business.

The Purpose of the Inventory

"The Inventory is to the stock record what counting the cash is to the cash register."

A CLERK in a retail dry goods store sold half a dozen items to a customer for cash. As he was wrapping up the order he slipped ten yards of silk into the package.

When he rang up the sale on the cash register it did not include the ten yards of silk.

The cash register didn't yell "murder," and there was no record of the silk removed from stock.

When the owner of the store counted his cash at night, he

"—slipped 10 yds. of silk—"

found in his cash register just the amount which the tape showed should be there.

He thought his clerks were all honest. He never suspected anything to the contrary. Yet this one clerk was as crooked as the negro porter's kinky hair.

At least a dozen of the customers of the store always insisted upon being waited on by this one clerk. Apparently it was friendship and good salesmanship. In reality, in this case, it was—something else.

These customers, apparently among the best customers of the store, came in almost every day. The amount of goods they took away unpaid for, and uncharged, however, much more than ate up the profit on the goods for which they paid.

At the end of the year an inventory was taken. But the method of taking inventory in this store wasn't designed to uncover crookedness. It was only designed

61

to give the owner of the store a rough *estimate* of the amount of goods on hand.

The inventory was not checked against the sales or purchases. No stock record was kept.

About three years after this clerk was employed the owner of the store decided that he should have a better bookkeeping system.

Within a month after the complete system was put in operation the crookedness of the clerk was discovered. The loss was estimated at $5000 a year through the dishonesty of this one clerk.

The merchant now takes an inventory four times a year and keeps a stock record which enables him to check his inventories against the stock he should have on hand. It protects him and his clerks.

His purchase record shows him the exact amount of stock bought of each line and of each division in each line—shirts of different sizes, for instance. When goods are sent from the stock room into the store, the amount is recorded in the stock book.

At the end of three months when the goods in the store are inventoried, the amount on hand in the store, and in the stock room, must balance with the stock as shown on the stock record.

His new bookkeeping system departmentizes his store in such a way that if any particular line of goods was short he could at once trace the shortage to the clerk who was in charge of that department.

A druggist in a little Pennsylvania town who had never taken an inventory in the ten years he had been in business, got pinched for money and decided to check up his stock in the hope of raising money by a clean up sale.

He found $15,000 worth more goods on his shelves than he thought he had.

He thought he was carrying about $10,000 worth of stock. In reality, he was carrying $25,000 worth. He had kept no records that enabled him to know how much he had purchased; how much goods he had sold; or the amount of profits he had made.

"—carrying heavy stock—"

If his store had burned out before taking his inventory he would have been satisfied with $10,000 from the insurance companies. He would not have known that he was figuring himself out of $15,000.

After he took his inventory he was so astonished at what he found that he decided to put in a system which would enable him to know exactly where he stood all the time.

With an accurate system he was soon able to reduce the amount of stock he carried and to make a great deal more money.

The amount of capital released by the up-to-date methods enabled him to meet his bills and open another store. Now he conducts half a dozen stores.

An inventory without a stock record affords no check against the goods which *should* show in the inventory. A stock record without an inventory affords no check against the theft of goods from stock.

The inventory is to the stock record what the counting of cash is to the cash register.

Running along from year to year without knowing what stock you have on hand is no more business-like than going along from day to day without knowing what money is in the cash drawer.

Are you only *guessing* at the amount of stock *you* have on hand? Is *your* inventory only an *estimate* of the amount of goods you *should* have.

Can you honestly say that you are able to make as much money out of your business without really *knowing* all there is to know about it, as you could make out of it if you *did* have the information at your fingers' ends. Be honest with yourself.

Frank L. Feisler, of Erie, Pa., is very enthusiastic about his system of accounting. A year ago he declared his old system was entirely adequate. No inducement would cause him to **go back** to it now.

"Weighing" Employees

"In scientifically managed stores, every
clerk is a sales Barometer whose readings
are always visible to the manager."

THE head of a big Chicago department store, looking over the sales figures for the month, noticed
that the clothing department showed a slight falling
off from the preceding month and from the correspond-
ing month of the preceding year.

On examining the reports
for the sales of each employee
in the department, he found that
three of them had made less
sales than during the preceding
month, or during the corres-
ponding month of the preced-
ing year.

A further study of the figures proved that these
three clerks had shown a steady falling off, while the
other two clerks in the same department had gradually
built up their sales.

The two clerks were costing about 8½ per cent on
their gross sales as against 9½ percent for the same
clerks for the preceding year, a nice increase in efficiency.

The other three clerks, who showed a falling off,
were costing around 11 to 12 per cent. That is, their
salaries equalled 11 to 12 per cent of their gross sales.

This brought the salary cost for the department up
to 10½ to 11 per cent of the sales.

It wasn't necessary for the manager to call in
the Department head. No conferences were necessary.
The figures told the whole story. Two of the five

"—Two clerks beat sales of three others—"

clerks were good clerks and three of the five were unprofitable, inefficient.

In a month the Department sales had picked up until the salary cost was down to the regular 9½ per cent—five good clerks were handling the sales.

In the big stores, clerks are judged and paid on a basis of the amount of goods they sell. If a clerk is paid $6 a week, she must sell goods to the aggregate of between $65 and $70 a week. That is, her salary cannot exceed 9½ per cent of her sales.

There is no *guess work* about the value of employees in the scientifically managed stores. Employees are judged wholly by what they do, and the figures which are furnished to the head of the store are figures which enable him to absolutely *know*, without a question of doubt, what every clerk is doing and what he is worth.

Every employee is a Barometer, whose readings, in dollars of sales and percent of cost, are always on file in the manager's office.

If the salary runs to 8 or 7 per cent the employee is scheduled for a raise. If it runs down to 5 or 4 per cent the employee will soon be promoted.

Have you ever puzzled over the problem of whether to raise the salary of a certain employee who is looking for a better job?

Have you ever wondered whether the old employee who seems satisfied to stay on with you year after year without much increase in salary is really worth what he is getting?

If you have more than one clerk, are you absolutely sure which is the *best* one?

Do you know whether one of them is making himself "solid" with your customers by giving them long measures and over-weights?

Do you know whether the clerk who sells most goods is really bringing in the *most profits* or just selling the goods that go *easiest?*

Wouldn't it put some warmth in your words when you tell John that you are going to give him that extra dollar a week he asked for, if you could turn to your records and see that John had been showing a steady increase in sales day by day and week by week for many months past?

And wouldn't it put backbone into your decision *not* to give Henry a raise when you could see by your records that his sales were showing a steady falling off? Maybe you could even find another "John" to take his place.

Let John and Henry make out a sales slip for each sale. Have the figures on these slips tabulated by days, then recapitulated into months. Then you can *know*, all the time, which is the *best* clerk.

It wouldn't take much time. The big stores find that it pays *big dividends* in "weighing" clerks, in the prevention of mistakes, in supplying information about sales by lines of goods, by clerks, etc.

It costs them as much per clerk as it would you. Some of them have as high as 5,000 clerks, all making out sales slips on every sale.

The average big store can find out more about the sales ability of any one of its 5,000 clerks in five minutes than the average small store could tell about its one clerk in a whole month.

The success of big stores proves that it *pays* to keep records. Are you going to let the big fellows crowd you out of business, or are you going to defend yourself with the weapons they have sharpened for you.

Moody & Moody, dry goods and clothing, and the Monroe Mercantile Co., grocers and butchers, are located on opposite sides of the street in Monroe, Wash. Both keep records which enable them to know where they stand, all the time.

Cutting the Delivery Cost
to One-third

"An organizer is better than a hard worker:
The man who wastes time over small things,
has little time to look after *big* things."

A LIVE retailer in the suburbs of Boston, found himself maintaining nine delivery wagons.

He could not afford that. It was eating up his profits. It was a big drag on his little business.

He set about investigating modern methods of delivery. He cut the number of wagons to four by solving his problem in this way:

"—high delivery expense.—"

A card was prepared and sent out to all customers explaining to them that by systematizing his delivery he had cut the expense of selling goods.

A cut in the expense meant smaller prices, a saving of money, to customers.

The delivery territory was divided into four districts and the number of deliveries cut to two a day.

Each customer received a card with her name written in, giving the hours of delivery for that district.

Several customers resented systematized delivery and threatened to quit if they could not get groceries at any hour of the day. The grocery man stood pat.

A few customers *did* quit, but when they came square up against the facts and found that systematized delivery *did* mean *better prices*, they forgot their desire for every-hour-service.

In a month they had all come back, with many

additional ones. They found that *they*, not the *grocer*, paid the delivery bills.

Every wagon left the store at 8 o'clock in the morning and at 1 o'clock in the afternoon.

Up to 8 o'clock the telephones were busy for morning deliveries. Later in the day they were busy for afternoon deliveries.

Each telephone order was considered exactly as an order given over the counter.

A sales slip was made out in duplicate, one copy going to the customer with the goods and the other going to the bookkeeper to be used in working the sales statement.

Drivers were given proper memorandum to enable them to make collections and to give the cashier a check on their collections.

This system worked so well and gave such satisfaction that the number of wagons has since been cut to three, with business continually increasing.

At $25 a week for each wagon that means a saving of $150 a week—more than $7,800 a year!

A grocer can't afford to deliver a can of corn "in a hurry, for dinner" without somebody paying the bill.

Even with systematized delivery the cost averages about five to six cents per order for delivery—about 1½ per cent of the gross sales.

The hurry-up order delivered separately costs a great deal more. *An unscientific delivery system may cost as high as 3 percent or 4 percent of the gross sales!*

"—in a hurry for dinner—"

Is the grocer going to add that to the cost of doing business, making somebody pay the bill?

If he does, that will increase his expenses and makes

it necessary for him to cut his profit or *raise his prices to everybody—that* will drive away business.

He cannot add it to each individual bill. That would surely drive away all his business, one customer at a time.

Any grocer who now maintains one delivery wagon can double or triple his delivery service by systematizing the delivery.

Any grocer who now has use for three delivery wagons can save the cost of two with scientific methods —he can save the expense of two delivery outfits—$30 to $60 a week.

System saves money. Systematizing *any* work reduces the expense of doing that work.

That deliveries can be systematized has been demonstrated by all big city stores—and by many *little* country stores.

The middle photo shows Howland, Texas, where the Howland Mercantile Company's store (shown in the top picture) is located. The lower photo shows the general store of J. E. Tull, Kennewick, Wash. Both of these are live stores.

Accounting Good at the Bank

"The sort of man the banks says *No* to
is the man who doesn't know all the
facts about his business."—*System*.

HENRY JOHNSON was a small grocer whose specialty was fresh eggs and good butter.

His trade increased under the stimulus of right methods and new clerks were employed. Finally his business reached a point where much larger quarters and better facilities were necessary.

He kept his own books, consisting of a daybook and a ledger and didn't see a need for anything better.

The time came, however, when more credit was needed to meet the demands of his increased business. He went to the bank to seek an accommodation.

His banker asked him for a statement of his affairs. Of course he was unable to give a satisfactory statement and the loan was deferred.

This was a rather rude awakening to the necessities of his business. He took the banker's advice and called in an auditor.

The auditor told him that it would be necessary to adapt his system of accounts to meet the changed conditions of his business.

His single-entry books had been all right to start with, but they were now too incomplete. The completing entries must be made at frequent and regular intervals.

Additional accounts had to be opened and the books kept in such a way that he could know at all times just where it stood.

In short, he needed to know as much about his

big business now as he *was* able to know about his business when it was *little*.

The auditor's advice was followed. The system recommended was installed, and a competent bookkeeper was put in charge.

Mr. Johnson soon realized that he could now do what he had long desired to do—branch out. It was no longer a necessity for him to be constantly on the job to know what was being done.

Today Mr. Johnson has a string of stores and is known as the "Grocery King" of his city.

He has long since ceased to be the sort of man the bank says *No* to. He knows the detail facts about his business so well that his bank has all kinds of confidence in him.

"—Grocery King—"

"There are lots of business men who don't really know much about their business—bright, industrious, business men," said a Banker.

"There's a popular notion that a man may be expected to know his own business. As a banker, I've grown skeptical about it.

"A man may be at his desk every day and not really know what's happening in his store.

"The thing that shows whether a business man's request for credit is right or not is the statement he shows you.

"Most banks now use special forms and reports that enable us to know the direction in which most of our prospective customers are going."

Every merchant keeps some kind of records. But most of them keep accounts which *don't account*.

Some merchants neglect to keep complete records because it costs money, *but they pay for the records anyway*, whether they keep them or not. In fact they pay most for the records they *don't* keep.

Doing without a thing which is *needed* does not save its cost. It always costs more to do without a thing which is really *needed* than the thing itself would cost.

W. D. Simmons, head of the great Simmons Hardware Company, tells the story of a retailer who went broke because he failed to realize the importance of being able at any time to show his creditors just how his business stood.

He didn't keep proper records of the details of his business. When he got into a close pinch and needed credit or additional capital he couldn't show his banker nor the supply house, any good reason why they should have confidence in him.

Things had gone so far before he really knew the conditions he was facing, that he couldn't possibly save himself. He was broke before he knew it.

"In talking with him, afterwards," said Mr. Simmons, "I found that he had thought if he kept track of his invoices until they were paid, so as to know how much he owed and to whom, and kept a record of the amount of money different people owed him, that was really all that was necessary.

"Any records other than those, he thought, were 'foolishness', and just made extra work."

Every merchant has an accounting

"—many stores for sale—"

system that *he* considers sufficient for his business. Most of them even think it the *best system that could be designed* for their business.

That is why so many retail stores are for sale—why only a bare 5% of all Retailers really make a success of their business.

That is why so many of them, like the hardware man Mr. Simmons tells about, are unable to get credit in a pinch.

As a test could you prepare a statement of your business on short notice that you, as a banker, would be willing to loan depositors' money on?

Could you produce a statement of your business in 24 hours that would convince a cold-blooded, hard-headed creditor that you really know your business?

If you can't, you may come down to the store some morning and find the sheriff ready to sell you out to satisfy some fool creditor to whom you can't *prove* that you are making money.

Storms break very quickly, sometimes. Be ready for yours when it comes.

The Boss' Eye

"YES, all these things are true," says the retailer, "but how am I going to stop these leaks. I may be so busy out on the sidewalk selling turnips that I don't know the molasses barrel is leaking in the cellar."

"—a system will not DO anything—"

That is just why this book was written. No proprietor who is selling on the sidewalk, or behind the counter for that matter, can keep track of all the leaks, unless he is in a one-man business and is selling everything for cash to those who carry the goods home.

Then, the goods on the shelves, and the cash in the bank and in the cash drawer, are his assets.

He may be able to sell the goods, or make a physical inventory, in a single day—and count his money in a few minutes.

What he *owes* are his *liabilities*.

Everything is under his own physical eye: he could tell in a short time just what he is worth.

When he begins selling on credit, enlarges his business by adding one or fifty or a hundred employees, buys goods that are stored below and above, and starts a delivery department, *then* he no longer has the business under his eye—the molasses barrel may empty itself without his being the wiser. Hence he must have a system that will keep a *record* of the *results* of all the activities of his people—of the incoming and outgoing of the goods (which represent his money) —that will tell him the true value of all this activity.

Any system is just a method by which the Boss may keep his eye on the results of his business. With an adequate system he can have in one place an accurate reflection of all that goes on in his business.

The boss may keep his eye on the results of his business

The system is an accounting system, because it *accounts* to him for every penny that he gets and every penny he pays out, in time, work or goods.

According to the thoroughness and efficiency of

the system in searching out and telling the whole truth about the activities of the business depends whether the Boss' Eye has a chance to see the things it ought to see.

If the System is right, then it is up to the *Eye* to see the facts, and the *Judgment* to use them.

The System will not *do* anything. It will only show the Eye what *ought to be done*.

It all comes back to the Boss with the Eye.

No matter how handsomely bound, or prettily ruled the pages of the account books—no matter how bright and new his pens and blotters, or how polished the cash register and how modern the adding machine—these alone won't make a business successful.

They are only the most efficient means by which to attain an end.

No matter, on the other hand, how clever the *merchant*—if he has no books of account, or if he has incomplete accounting books and inefficient methods of handling them, he can't make the profits of the man who is his equal in merchandising ability and who has a thorough system, efficiently handled.

All businesses are "different"—because each one has an individuality—just as all horses are "different," but there are certain horse qualities common to all.

So all retail businesses are alike in the things which make them retailers and not manufacturers, or railroads or even wholesalers.

All accounting principles are the same—always: but the methods of applying them may vary.

You may have loose-leaf books or card-ledgers, but your debit and credit will be the same: you may use a cash register, but you'll have to have a double entry set of books, or your credit won't be as good as the credit of the man who *does* have such a set of books.

Assets

Horses & Wagons
Furniture & Fixtures
Inventory of Stock (By Depts.)
Freight on Purchases (By Depts)
Customers Ledger Controlling
    Account
  (Individual accounts may be kept in
  the same binder with the general
  ledger, but should be grouped by
  themselves.)
Bills Receivable
Cash in Bank
Petty Cash
Prepaid Insurance
Proprietor's Personal Account

Liabilities

Capital Account
Audited Vouchers
  (Controlling Voucher
  Record.)
Accounts Payable
  (Controlling Individual
  Accounts of Shippers.)
Accrued Taxes
Bills Payable
Reserved for Doubtful
    Accounts
Reserved for Depreciation
Profit & Loss

Expense Accounts

Salaries
Rent, Light & Heat
Store Supplies
Advertising
Insurance
    { These Accounts to be kept by Departments
Stable Expense
Printing & Stationery
Postage
Telephone & Telegraph
Discounts, Allowances &
    Exchange
Bad Debts
Taxes
Depreciation
Miscellaneous Expense

Revenue Accounts

Sales & Cost of Sales
  (By Departments.)
Cash Discounts Received
Other Income (Itemize.)

The other day a retailer who had been doing a fair business, said: "My business has been increasing right along year after year, and very much more than expenses have increased. So it seems to me, that I ought to be making quite a little more money than I am."

He consulted an old business friend about it.

They looked over his books, which had been carefully kept by a young man who had "picked up bookkeeping."

It soon appeared that the retailer's books were not kept so he could show how the gross profits of any month compared with any other month. The books could not show for any particular period whether expenses had increased out of proportion to other things.

Then his friend's expert bookkeeper was put to work—and he soon found that a trusted employee had been stealing the profits.

The *ineffective* accounting method couldn't show that fact—therefore the Boss' Eye could not see it.

It is not the purpose of this little book to show a retailer how to install a system of accounts. He should have that done for him by a man who studies his business and its requirements. It is our purpose to show him *why* he should have all the facts.

On page 80 is shown a list of accounts which a retailer who rents his store, makes his own deliveries and has, or has not, a perpetual detailed inventory, must have, to intelligently manage his business.

This list is offered merely to show the kinds of information which a retailer must have to be safe.

Remember, there are three things you *must* answer:

1—Where is your cash and how much have you?

2—How much do you owe?

3—Where's the stock you bought, how much have you sold, and how much have you on your shelves?

If you have a system of accounts that tell you these things, you have:

1—Protected yourself in *knowing* what you are *doing* and by knowing the *value* of your activity.

2—Protected your family—your wife and children —so when you are called away, your administrator or executor won't have to report that "he left his estate in a badly tangled condition." Neither will they lose through most of what you leave being eaten up in the process of untangling of your affairs.

3—Protected yourself against fire loss, because without a system of accounts you would probably be unable to prove more than 60 or 70 percent of your loss.

4—Given yourself a chance to use all the credit you are entitled to at the bank, by having an accounting system that shows what you are doing, and that *you know* what you are doing.

Now, get started right on this matter of an accounting system.

Don't fool with make-shift systems—short cut ideas that cut the essential facts out of the statements you get.

A great manufacturer of accounting systems largely used by retailers wrote the writer the other day:

"I have from my experience come to know that the rank and file of small retail merchants care little or nothing about system in their business, and this accounts for the large proportion of failures. Even after we succeed in installing one of our systems very few of them will use it correctly; therefore, their success with it is limited. They merely want a system or device that will relieve them of the bookkeeping, yet they are not willing to do the little extra work necessary to compile the comparative statements of their business which would enable them to more intelligently determine just what progress they are making."

Get the facts. Hire a bookkeeper *who knows how* to help you. Get started right. Then have an expert come in once in a while (say every three months) and check up your work—just to keep you on the right track.

Then keep your Eye on the Expense and Income accounts.

When the former jumps, dig into it and find out *why*.

When the latter decreases, dig again and find the reason; when it increases, find out what produces the effect, and push that good thing for all you are worth.

Keep your Eye on the facts of the business. It can't see too many, and you can't know too much about what those facts really mean.

That is why the big business has an accounting system: and why no permanently successful business, big or little, has ever gotten along without an adequate bookkeeping system.

No business man has ever been a *failure* because he *had* a bookkeeping system. No business man has ever been *successful* because he *didn't have* one.

L. C. Thayer's booth in one of the Boston Markets is so small he has limited his office to 3x4 feet and operates his adding machine on a shelf. The lower picture was taken through a window because it was too small to get the camera into. It shows the office of A. C. Candor, hardware, of Lock Haven, Pa.

Paying For What You
Don't Get

"If a man needs a thing in his business,
it is likely to cost more not to supply the
need than the thing itself would cost."

A DRUMMER, walking into a hardware and implement store in the corn belt, found the proprietor
back in the warehouse setting up a stove.

After watching the
work for a few minutes
the drummer interrupted
him.

"There's a chance for
a man to get a good place
as manager of a big store
down the state, " he be-

"—boss setting up a stove—"

gan. 'It's owned by a stock company. At present
they're without a manager."

"The position will pay $200 a month to the right
man. I'd like to find some hustling fellow I could
put them in touch with. They're good customers of
the house."

"Say, that looks good to *me!*" the merchant re-
turned. "You know I've found it pretty hard here,
for lack of capital. *I* wouldn't mind *making a change*
if I could get a place like *that.*"

"Do you consider yourself a $200 man?" the
drummer asked, with a twinkle in his eye.

"I certainly do!"

"Well, *you* wouldn't do at all. That company
wouldn't stand for a manager who spends his time

putting up stoves while a $60 clerk is out in the store trying to sell a hard customer."

The drummer may have been only joshing about the $200 job to teach the hardware man a lesson, but the story has a point just the same.

A man who allowed himself a salary of $200 a month was doing his own bookkeeping by hand.

He spent two hours a day on his books, not including the monthly trial balance.

At that rate it cost him about $1.75 a day, $45 a month, to keep his books.

He bought a Burroughs Bookkeeping Machine. Immediately he cut the amount of the time required to one-half. This gave him even better records at a cost of less than $25 a month.

This is a saving of $20 a month, $240 in a year. Before his Burroughs wears out, that saving, deposited regularly in a savings bank, would aggregate more than $6,000.

But that is not *all* this man saved.

He found that he could get a girl to keep his books *on the machine* as good as *he* could keep them by hand.

Working full time she cost him but $1.50 a day and gave him so much valuable information that he soon *doubled his business*.

A man is not in business to *keep books*, any more than he is in business to sweep out his store. He is in business to *sell goods*.

Books are kept to give him, every day, a complete statement of his business, so that he may know what steps to take to sell *more* goods profitably.

When a man is cooped up, in his bookkeeping cage, who is running the business for him? It is being run by his cheap clerks.

Can a $60 a month clerk run a business as well as a $200 proprietor?

Of course not. When the business is being run by a $60 man, it is a $60 business. When it is run by a $200 man it is a $200 business.

That is the difference. A $200 man can sell *more* goods. He will drive away *less* regular customers. He can convert more of the *transient* customers into *regular* customers.

If he is a $200 man he can *use* more of the *figure-information* shown by the bookkeeper—if he saves the one hour to *think* in and saves his mind fresh to work out ways of increasing his business.

One new customer added to a store's regular patronage every day, means an increase in gross business which at the end of a year would amount to $1500 a week—$63,000 a year.

Five per cent net profit on that volume of business will buy a mighty fine automobile.

One new customer

If the proprietor of a store who keeps his own books by hand, would save the time which he can save by using a Burroughs and devotes that time to *thinking* out schemes for window displays and advertising, and *planning* sales and better interior arrangements, and *working* to put his schemes and plans into use, couldn't he bring in one new customer a day?

Couldn't he make his business pay him several times more than a Burroughs would cost?

If he couldn't, he *isn't* a $200 man.

If *you* can save one little ten minutes every day and use that ten minutes to *think* with, *you* can increase *your* business enough to pay for several book-keeping machines in one year.

You could get along without scales, if you and your customers were satisfied to *guess* at *weights*.

You can get along without a Burroughs if you are satisfied to *guess* at the *figure facts* about your business, or if you are satisfied to *pay the extra cost* of getting those figure facts with a pencil.

You may not realize it, but it is no less *un*profitable to go on paying in *leaks* and *losses* and other ways for a Burroughs you are *not* using when it would cost you much *less* to *use* one.

Talk the proposition over with a Burroughs man. Let him explain to you how it is now costing you more *not* to use a Burroughs than it would cost you to buy and use one.

One hour of your time invested in a little business talk of this kind will be worth a considerable sum to you, even if you don't decide to use a Burroughs.

The Burroughs man, who will call when you say the word, has talked with hundreds of other business men—knows how *they* solved *their* problems—knows how to apply *their* successful methods to *your* business.

Will you talk with him about it—without cost or obligation to you?

Keeping Books with a Machine

What The Burroughs Is

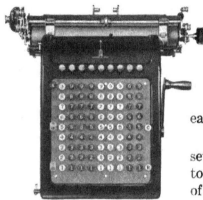

Each row contains all the figures from 1 to 9—allowing the use of all the fingers at once.

THE Burroughs is a machine to handle all kinds of figures, in any way it is desired to handle them.

It is about the size of a typewriter, but very much easier to operate.

The keyboard consists of several rows of keys—from 6 to 17, depending upon the size of the machine.

Each row contains all the figures from 1 to 9—ciphers print automatically where needed.

The rows are arranged in such a way that any figure can be printed in any column by simply touching the right key.

It writes down figures just as much more rapidly, just as much more legibly, than they can be written down by hand, as a typewriter writes letters more rapidly and more legibly than they could be written by hand.

It automatically adds *all* the figures it writes down, and is ready at any time, by the mere operating of a handle, to *record*, without the possibility of error, the absolutely correct total of all the figures written—a total which has been accumulated in the machine during the writing operation.

After a few minutes practice anybody can put figures into the machine faster than they could be written with a pencil. Any intelligent operator can soon learn to use *all* the fingers of both hands.

Touching keys writes the figures, three or four at a time.

The adding or calculating is entirely automatic. When a key is depressed it remains down until the operating handle is pulled.

The pulling of the handle causes all keys to assume their original position and the amount of the number to be printed on the paper and totalled on the adding wheels.

When all the numbers are in the machine, depressing the total button while pulling the handle causes the total, which has accumulated on the adding wheels, to be printed at the bottom of the column on the sheet —or in any other desired place on the sheet.

With every machine is furnished an instruction book, which explains in simple language and with

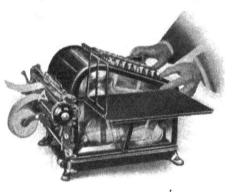

Obtaining the total; takes but a second for any length of column.

many illustrations how anybody can do a hundred things with the machine that the average person wouldn't think of trying to do without the instruction book.

How The Burroughs Is Used

Here are a few of the things for which Burroughs Machines are being used by thousands of retailers:

Making up a daily record of sales by clerks, by departments and by lines of goods, from sales slips.

Reconciling bank balances by listing outstanding checks.

Checking freight and cartage bills.

Handling deposit tickets in duplicate.

Auditing and checking cash book.

Auditing ledger.

Tabulating cost and selling price of articles sold.

Compiling expenses by different lines of goods and by departments.

Totaling and balancing outstanding accounts.

Making records of C. O. D. orders.

Handling records of petty cash.

Balancing daily cash books.

Proving daily postings, which guarantees a balance.

Making out and proving monthly statements.

Compiling a record of purchases by lines of goods and by departments.

Handling stock records and inventories.

Auditing charge systems.

Checking invoices.

Checking vouchers and making voucher records.

A time-saving, mistake preventing, worry-eliminating brain assistant for the retailer or his bookkeeper. This machine, or any one of the 85 other Burroughs, can be used on a high stand at the bookkeeper's desk or on a low stand beside the manager's desk.

Burroughs Systems Service

Across the street, perhaps is a merchant you've never visited—across the state, several you've never heard of.

EVER since the Burroughs Company was organized, twenty years ago, its men have been in close contact with the planning and accounting end of thousands of business houses.

Naturally they have learned a great many things about the best accounting methods in use in every line of business.

The Burroughs Department of Systems Service was organized for the purpose of boiling down this information, and to put it into shape to be distributed to other business men interested in it.

A few years ago, the now famous Burroughs Book, "A Better Day's Work," was written

"—boiling down experience into systems books—"

from this boiled down experience. Four large editions, 135,000 copies, of this book have gone out to business men in all parts of the world.

Another book, called "Cost Keeping Short Cuts," adopted as a text book in the Universities of Wisconsin, Indiana and Minnesota and in other big schools —originated in the same way.

After these two books were written, it was decided that there should be something especially designed for the Retailer. A book which we called, "Why Don't you Go home" was written and published.

The book was so well received that when the first edition of 25,000 copies was exhausted, it was decided to re-issue the book along a little more complete lines.

The result was *this* Retail book, "A Better Day's Profits," probably the most unusual book of its kind ever published.

Naturally the men who use Burroughs Bookkeeping machines are progressive men. The fact that they use machines proves that they are always in search of the *best methods*.

Nearly 150,000 of these business men are always ready and willing to explain their best methods to us, in exchange for the methods which we have gathered from thousands of other business men. For that reason it is easy for us to obtain information that could not possibly be obtained in any other way.

It would require hundreds of men many months to visit as many modern business houses as the Burroughs organization has visited.

In reading this book, you will find many things that will strike you as very unusual. Possibly some things you will find hard to believe. But if you could take the time, and cared to assume the expense, to visit 150,000 business houses, in every part of  the world, *you* would find many things that would surprise you.

"—will strike you as unusual.—"

In addition to the information which we have collected first hand, through the personal contact of our large organization, from other business houses all over the world, we have also collected a vast amount of information by mail.

For instance the chapter on figuring profits, in

this book, is based on an extensive investigation to determine how retailers figure their profits.

The results of the investigation were very interesting; in fact they were so interesting that several hundred retail trade papers printed a story of the investigation as news.

All the other chapters in the book are based upon information and experience which is not available to the ordinary publisher of books. This fact will probably account, in some measure at least, for its being "different" from other books.

In this book we have only tried to drive home, in a graphic way, the possibilities of better bookkeeping; to make retailers want more information; to make them see and understand that they can only succeed by basing their efforts upon real information and directing their energies from positive knowledge rather than from guess.

The Department of Systems Service does not undertake to install bookkeeping systems. It offers only a suggestion service. The members of its staff do not pose as Public Accountants, nor as Experts.

It has nothing to sell. It does not buy anything. It is just a department for the collection and distribution of ideas that help the users of Burroughs machines to use their machines to better advantages, and to help business men find out how they can adapt Bookkeeping machines to their work.

The service of this department is available to any business man who is interested in better Bookkeeping methods, whether they use Burroughs Bookkeeping machines or not.

Personality in Business

YOU may learn from competitors, whether they be in the Mail Order business or conducting a cross-roads store. Here is one of the secrets of success of a firm which is a competitor of every Retail Store in America.

NO matter how large the business grows, it is always an expression of personal force, just as the personal force of a nation is the sum total of the personal force of its people.

We believe that our customers and employees feel that our business is as much a matter of personality today as it was in the beginning. Behind each transaction is personal guarantee, and we trust that behind each customer is personal interest in the growth and the perfecting of a system that seeks to interpret the personal desire of each man, woman or child who deals with it.

Thus its policy is a composite of the ideas of all its customers, expressing their will in all its undertakings, while its increase, growth and success are, we believe, as much matters of personal pride and gratification to our patrons as they are to ourselves and our employees.

—A. MONTGOMERY WARD

Form 1531A-25M-5-19-C. A. Co